manglo saxon

*Marvelously Mangled
Meanings for
Well-Worn Words*

R. S. Young

Pomegranate

SAN FRANCISCO

Published by Pomegranate Communications, Inc.
Box 808022, Petaluma, CA 94975-8022
800 227 1428; www.pomegranate.com

Pomegranate Europe Ltd.
Unit 1, Heathcote Business Centre
Hurlbutt Road
Warwick, Warwickshire CV34 6TD, U.K.
44 1926 430111

While it is the author's original work, *Manglo Saxon* contains certain expressions and phrases commonly used in various countries. To the best of the author's knowledge and belief, this text does not infringe upon any existing copyright, and any such infringement would be entirely unintentional and incidental only to the work as a whole.

Library of Congress Cataloging-in-Publication Data

Young, R. S. (Richard Stephen), 1961–
    Manglo-Saxon : marvelously mangled meanings for well-worn words / R. S. Young.
        p. cm.
    ISBN 0-7649-2737-X
        1. English language—Terms and phrases—Humor.
2. English language—Humor. 3. Vocabulary—Humor. I. Title.
PN6231.W64Y68 2003
428.1'02'07—dc22

                                        2003053683

Pomegranate Catalog No. A694
Designed by Jamison Design, Nevada City, California
Printed in China

13 12 11 10 09 08 07 06 05 04   10 9 8 7 6 5 4 3 2 1

Contents

The great American lexicographer

Noah Webster (1758–1843) sought to change the spelling of many English words so that they look the way they sound. If the concept were taken one step further, could English words be made to mean the way they look and sound?

The only way to find out was by performing an experiment in which common English words were redefined with linguistic rigour.

This experiment resulted in the sublimely logical neo-language called Manglo-Saxon. While some words' traditional pronunciation was necessarily sacrificed in the service of logic, British English—where it diverges from New World usage, as in the case of British "shedyool" vs. American "skedjul"—has been retained out of respect for the ancient wellspring of today's global lingua franca. In purely vocabularian terms, some entries may puzzle American readers. These are distinguished by a special symbol and are explained in notes called *To the Puzzled American Reader;* read further for an expanded discussion.

The experimental team decided to leave in occasional stretches of logic; these were allowed to survive in the spirit of innovation that characterizes that most living of languages, English, and also as a form of limbering system and aerobic exercise. Not one team member had an overweight brain when the experiment concluded.

NB: In a number of cases, the pronunciation has been scientifically improved during the original word's transmogrification into Manglo-Saxon. You, reader, may have to step back, take a long look, and perhaps try a few alternative stresses and/or vowel trades (long for short or vice versa) to make sense of the exquisitely sensible new word.

A ‡ means that the old word and/or the thing or activity or concept it describes may be unknown to the non-British reader. This reader may expect to find an explanatory note elsewhere on the page.

We here present our findings, with examples of usage in the tradition of Doctor Johnson, whose *Dictionary of the English Language* (1755) remains an inspiration to all those who love words.

Manglo-Saxon
for Epicures

Aquaplane:

Nonsparkling spring water.

"The surf and turf for me, please. And could we have a little aquaplane?"

Avoirdupois:

In possession of peas.

"Am I to assume from the weight of the shucks in your pockets that I've caught you avoirdupois?"

Baltimore‡:

A second-year student curry chef.

"*Isn't he a freshman in that school of Indian cuisine in Maryland?*" "*No, Baltimore.*"

Bollard:

Fat extracted from weevils.

"*If you're overweight, you've got to find a way to avoid that bollard.*"

Cannibals:

Snacks for the restroom.

"*Is there any food in the house?*" "*Try the john, I think there's cannibals in there!*"

---

‡ *To the Puzzled American Reader:* **Baltimore**: balti is curry.

3

Canoodling:

Eating tinned spaghetti.

"When I suggest an Italian restaurant, he says he'd rather stay home canoodling with me."

Casualty:

An informal early-evening meal.

"It won't be a full-dress surgeons' dinner; we'll just tuck into a casualty."

Chevrolet:

With goat's milk.

"Would you like that chevrolet?" "No, thank you. I prefer black."

Cubicle:

An ice cube.

"I'll try one of those Shirley Temples. Do you have any cubicles?"

Decaffeinate:

To move up market and become a small restaurant.

"If we want a less rowdy clientele, we must decaffeinate."

Eightsome:

Consumed an amount.

"Eightsome. That's right, officer. Four women and four men downed half of our buffet, then ran."

Equator:

Exclamation on finding something unexpected in restaurant food.

"Equator! There's a spider in my soup."

Garrotes:

Carrots grown in garages.

"I've gotta string up some vegetables. Have you got any more of those garrotes?"

Hamlet:

A small pig.

"Come here, my little hamlet, prince of porkers. I'm going to turn you into Danish bacon."

Hamster:

One who enjoys pork products.

"He eats a dozen Scotch eggs‡, then works his flab off on the treadmill. The guy's a trueborn hamster."

Hashish:

Descriptor for a dish made with potatoes and corned beef.

"I don't know what he had in that frying pan, but it smelled kinda like hashish."

---

‡ *To the Puzzled American Reader:* Scotch egg: a hard-boiled egg plastered with sausage meat, rolled in crumbs, and fried.

Hebrew:

A man who makes tea or beer.

"It's thirsty work being lost in this desert. I could do with meeting a Hebrew."

Helpmeet:

A spicy seasoning blend.

"My chop hath no savor without my helpmeet."

Indelible:

Suitable for specialist food shops.

"Excellent curry sauce! It's absolutely indelible."

Jacobean:

A coffee type supposedly favored
by Michael Jackson.

"Is this freshly ground? It tastes ancient."
"Oh, maybe it's Jacobean."

Jargon:

A glass container when absent.

*"Now where am I gonna put my freakin' fruit
preserve?" "Why, where's your jargon?"*

Kerchief:

The man in charge of the
cherry brandy.

*"Don't worry, the kerchief will soon
mop that little spillage up."*

Lambasted:

A mutton joint immersed in its juices.

"My beef was with him. He chewed me out. I got lambasted."

Locality:

A slimmer's beverage.

"I need some sugar, but I don't think there is any in this locality."

Marmalade:

Soda made from marmots.

"Why all the rodents in the blender?"
"I'm making marmalade."

Marsupial:

An ingredient that spoils the flavor of the broth.

"This consommé tastes funny, I'm afraid there's a marsupial in it."

Parrots:

Hybridized vegetables resulting from crossing carrots with parsley.

"Nice green parrots, very crisp."

Prima donna‡:

A first-class kebab.

"It's white and red, like a prima donna covered in chili sauce."

---

‡ *To the Puzzled American Reader:* Donna: a donna, donah, or doneh kebab is spiced ground lamb on a skewer.

Pulsated:

Having had sufficient peas or beans.

"Honestly, I couldn't eat another thing. My stomach's just pulsated."

Qualitative:

Adjective describing the best potatoes.

"These are King Edwards and these are Maris Piper, but there's no qualitative difference."

Recruit:

To add condiments again.

"That should be enough oil and vinegar."
"If I were you, I'd recruit some more."

Rueful:

Having eaten sufficient marsupials.

"After downing three joeys, the swagman had a rueful look about him."

Salami:

A charitable, evangelistic organization of religious sausages.

"What's that music?" "It's the salami band in the deli."

Servitude:

To present already-masticated food.

"Servitude? I should think they'll choke on it."

Underground:

Inadequately crushed.

"Does this pabulum seem gritty to you?"
"Yes, as if it's been underground!"

Yom Kippur:

An expression of enthusiasm for smoked herrings.

"What's for supper on this Day of Atonement?" "Yom Kippur."

The **ANIMAL KINGDOM**

BALCONY:

An Eastern European rabbit.

"Either there are fluffy pom-poms on his slippers or he's standing on a balcony."

BASSOON:

An ape that can play a Fender guitar.

"Does his repertoire include swing?" "Are you kidding? He's a bassoon!"

BEAGLE:

A flying creature that nests in an eyrie and makes honey.

"Are those birds, bees, or planes? "I think it's two beagles having a dogfight."

CATASTROPHE:

Award for the best feline posterior.

"That Siamese on the winner's plinth is just waiting for a catastrophe."

DEFOLIANT:

A contraceptive for horses.

"The herd hasn't grown since I started spraying the paddock with defoliant."

DORMANT:

A small hymenopterous insect found in sleeping quarters.

"Is it an active termite nest?" "No, I'd say it's a dormant dormant nest."

ENDORSE:

To have a pony put down.

"The vet says we should have Prince destroyed, but I just can't endorse him."

FOIBLES:

Hairy agglomerates ejected by Brooklyn, New York, felines.

"For Chrissakes, da cat keeps coughin' up foibles."

17

GAMMON:

Fish found near nuclear power stations.

"I'll just cast my line here by the reactor and haul me out some gammon."

GANGLION:

A feline pride member.

"What's that?" "It just looks like a lump." "Is it a lone leopard?" "No, I think it's a ganglion."

GNOME:

The sort of grassland where the deer and the antelope and the gnu live.

"Gnome, gnome on the range."

HIPPOCAMPUS:

University for large African quadrupeds.

"Do they learn to swim, or is it instinctive?"
"It's all taken care of at the hippocampus."

HOSPITAL:

Equine saliva.

"Don't put your hand in his mouth or you'll find yourself in hospital."

ILLEGAL:

A diseased bird of prey.

"You'll have to quarantine that sick foreign bird. It's an illegal immigrant."

KIDNEY:

The patella of a young goat.

"Not bad. It's got chewy bits and crunchy bits. What is it?" "Steak and kidney pie."

LACTEAL:

To be without ducks.

"We've got milk for our coffee but nothing to shoot at. Looks like we lacteal."

LIMPET:

A sedated domestic animal.

"A simple pill turns a hysterical schnauzer into a wobbling limpet."

MANDOLIN:

A mythical beast, half human, half scaly anteater.

"It sounded like an aardvark, but maybe it was a mandolin."

NINCOMPOOPS:

The guano of the nincom bat.

"Watch out for those batty guys or you're going to get covered in nincompoops."

OSTRACIZED:

As big as an ostrich.

"Look at the length of that guy's neck. He's ostracized!"

OXYGENATED‡:

To be well informed about cows.

"He don't know nothin' about dairy herds. My fish are more oxygenated than he is."

PANDEMONIUM:

A room where Chinese bears can voice complaints.

"Pandemonium in there, that's what the zookeeper said."

QUARREL:

A flying rodent resulting from crossing a squirrel with a quail.

"I'd breed these two only I might start a quarrel."

---

‡ *To the Puzzled American Reader:* Oxygenated: "gen" is "information" in colloquial British English.

RELEGATE:

(Of a dog) The act of savaging a human shin repeatedly.

"It bit me before my last squash match and I don't want to be relegated."

SNIPPET:

To trim the hair of a domestic animal.

"That dog's coat's too long, I'm going to have to snippet."

THESAURUS:

The definitive dinosaur.

"Homework is to describe T. rex. Should I look in this Roget's thing?" "I'd try thesaurus."

WAGON:

A dog that has had its tail docked.

"These long-tailed dogs are easy to sell, but it's hard to shift them wagons."

X-RAY:

A dead flatfish.

"I swear it was a ghost fish, man, it swam right through me like some kind of x-ray."

YANKEE:

A dog on a leash.

"I knew a man in New England as used to drag his spaniel round on a leash. Sad little Yankee!"

PROFESSIONS
and PROCLIVITIES

ANATOMIST:

A writer of large books about mosquitoes.

"Those larvae could be of interest to an anatomist."

APOLOGIST:

A defender of the space program.

"I though he wouldn't support the expenditure, but he's an apologist."

ARGONAUTS:

Slang speakers.

"He says he's looking for a golden fleece, but with these argonauts that could mean anything."

BADGER:

A dispenser of badges.

"I've never seen so many creatures with labels on them. This forest must be full of badgers."

BALLYHOO:

A little-known dancer.

"Dame Margot was off color, so there was a ballyhoo."

BARBARIAN:

A hairdresser to the master race.

"I need to have it cut, Klaus, but I can't find a barbarian to do it for me."

BARRISTER:

One who engages in arm wrestling in drinking dens.

"I thought he was respectable?" "Oh no, he's a barrister!"

BRILLIANTINE:

An adolescent prodigy.

"This Elvis impersonator is a brilliantine. He makes your hair stand on end."

CADET:

A trainee rotter.

"Why not join up, Madam, it's a great life in the army." "Don't trust him, Minnie, he's a cadet."

CONDESCENDING:

Adjective related to early Australian colonists.

"I don't like the people in Port Arthur. They're condescending."

DECORATION:

A speech made by a captain to his crew.

"To recognise your bravery in action, I'm giving you all this decoration."

DIPLOMA:

The mother of all limbo dancers.

"I've never seen a girl get under a bar so low. She must have a diploma."

DUMPLING:

An abandoned child.

"Is it true you're not my real Mommy?"
"Well, yes, my little dumpling."

EDITOR:

A cockney boxer.

"You've got a lot of fan mail. Look at all these letters to the editor."

EXPENSIVE:

The condition of having sworn off thinking.

"I used to be careful with his money, but now I'm expensive and I don't give it a thought."

EXPUNGE:

To wean someone away from relying on others' charity.

"We can't let him borrow from everyone. We need to expunge him."

FEELINGS:

Salaried workers.

"It took hundreds of hired hands to build the Taj Mahal. He loved her. He paid for those feelings."

FOLIO:

Someone pretending to have been born between July 24 and August 23.

"Look at this folio, he's clearly Taurus."

GOBLET:

A noisy child.

"Sorry about the cacophony, I just knocked a goblet across the room."

HEADHUNTER:

One in search of the ship's toilets.

"See that guy on the main deck talking to the janitor? He's a headhunter."

KIDNAPPING:

A sleeping child.

"I thought you said you'd seen an abduction at the nursery." "No, I said a kidnapping."

KIPPER‡:

One who sleeps.

"He's not up yet. Soundest kipper I've ever seen."

LARGESSE:

A big woman.

"Generally I didn't think much of him, but I was certainly impressed by his largesse."

---

‡ *To the Puzzled American Reader:* **Kip:** British for sleep.

LENS:

Belonging to Len.

"What's that, your camera bag?" "No, lens case."

LIKELIHOOD:

A probable thug.

"Someone'll mug you. Like that guy on the corner with the scar on his nose. That's the likelihood around here."

LOBSTER:

One who tends to discard things.

"There's no point in giving him expensive gifts when you know he's a lobster."

MAISONETTE:

A female stone carver.

"*I wanted to settle down with a sculptress in a garret, but I guess I can live with a maisonette.*"

MILDEW:

A condensation problem at a cereal mill.

"*I'm sorry production is down, but we're having trouble with the mildew.*"

NANKEEN:

An enthusiastic grandmother.

"*Personally I didn't think much of that yellow cloth, but hell was nankeen.*"

NATURALIST:

A student of flying pests in the Russian mountains.

"Interested in insects, Boris? Why not become a naturalist."

NEWTONIAN:

A new arrival at Eton.

"On open day in the science block, old Etonians and Newtonians mingle."

PONTIAC:

A French bridge fetishist.

"Jeez, you don't ever want to drive through Paris with a Pontiac."

PYGMY‡:

A self-indulgent person.

"I'd love some more of that shortbread. I'm a bit of a pygmy."

QUASAR:

One who gives the appearance of being Russian royalty.

"Vladimir thinks he's a red star, but I'd say he's a quasar."

SEWER:

One who takes legal action for damages.

"He swears he's taking me to court. He always did have a mouth like a sewer."

---

‡ *To the Puzzled American Reader:* Pygmy: Like Cajun Americans, Cockney Britons sometimes append "me" to a self-descriptive declaration. A Cockney announcing his intention to drop in at the pub might say, "I'm off down the boozer, me."

SUFFRAGETTE:

One who experiences airport noise pollution.

"She voted against another runway. She was a suffragette."

TANGENT:

A man who has been out in the sun.

"I thought it was a sign of hot weather but no, it was a tangent."

TEMPLATE:

A tardy secretary.

"Ten past nine. You'll have to cut this out. I can't afford to have another template."

TERMITE:

School boarder who doesn't go home until the end of the semester.

"Smithers is looking antsy." "Yes, he's a termite."

THERMOCOUPLE:

Two people with a flask of hot coffee.

"Honey, I'm freezing. What wouldn't I give to be like that thermocouple."

UMLAUT:

An indecisive yob.

"You would have thought that a Mötorhead fan would know an umlaut when he saw one."

WINDLASS:

A flatulent Scotswoman.

"Why haul it up with a traction engine? It's noisier and smellier than a windlass."

IRRITANT:

Mother's annoying sister.

"If old Minnie's coming to visit, I'm taking a walk. She's a real irritant."

CORNICE:

Sister's daughter with the troublesome feet.

"She cringes every time she has to get up and leave her pillar. Poor cornice!"

VENTILATOR:

To complain at length.

"Avoid her like the plague. She'll start grousing now and ventilator."

YAMMER:

A vendor of sweet potatoes.

"I can't hear myself think. Go dismantle those market stalls and hush up that yammer."

Manglo-Ministry of Transport

Cantankerous:

Adjective describing an inability to tether a vessel to the seabed.

"If you're going to be so cantankerous, we'll end up on the rocks."

Carotid:

A rusty automobile.

"See sculptures welded from old vehicle parts at our local gallery, the Carotid Artery."

Carpet:

A nodding dog or similar mascot found on the parcel shelf of a vehicle.

"Her Majesty has a red carpet in her Rolls."

Decagon:

A recently departed London bus.

"I ran round ten sides of this weird-shaped bus depot only to find the decagon."

Giblets:

Small triangular sails.

"The guys on that boat are chicken. They haven't even got their giblets out."

Incarceration:

A sharp edge within a vehicle.

"Careful when you're welding those seams. I don't want to see any incarcerations."

Incarnation:

The United States of America.

"It lives, it breathes, but it doesn't walk. It's the one true incarnation."

Kaleidoscope:

TV coverage of a stretch of road known for its multicar accidents.

"Just look at the kaleidoscope! All those different colors smashing together."

Keeping:

Noise made when you lock the car by remote control.

"Just keeping it safe."

Khakis:

Devices for locking and unlocking automobiles.

"Where are my other trousers? I can't find my khakis."

Limit:

To travel by limousine.

"Why limit yourself when you can take a taxi with me?"

Nitrate:

The amount charged by taxis after dark.

"At dusk I brought the fertilizer home by cab. The nitrate was expensive."

Nitrogen‡:

Information for nocturnal oarsmen.

"I'm not taking a boat into a darkened atmosphere like that without nitrogen."

Quatrain:

Means of transporting plum-sized orangelike fruit.

"There were four lines at the station, but not a quatrain in sight."

---

‡ *To the Puzzled American Reader:* Nitrogen: as discussed in the note attending "Oxygenated," "gen" is "information" among the British.

Servile:

To behave like a flight attendant.

"Your duties will require you to be assertive and also servile number one."

Undertaker:

One who passes on the inside lane.

"I'm hardly moving. An undertaker just went by me in the slow lane. In a hearse."

Vanguard:

A security vehicle driver.

"You take out the vanguard, I'll deal with the van."

Vanish:

Somewhat like a van.

"What's he done to that car now? I've seen it looking weird before, but I've never seen it vanish."

Verger:

A roadside vendor.

"I took the main route through the church-yard and bought some grass from a verger there."

Wagon-lit:

A train on fire.

"It was a darned good job I wasn't asleep when I found myself aboard this wagon-lit."

Health Care

Analyst:

A proctologist.

"These psychotics are a pain in the backside. They need a psychiatrist and I need an analyst."

Balinese‡:

Inflammation of the patella caused by praying to Phoenician gods.

"They're all knobbly, like Balinese."

---

‡ *To the Puzzled American Reader:* Balinese: Baal: a Canaanite/Phoenician deity. "Bally": a euphemism for "bloody."

Bedeviled:

Having an aching back.

"I could hardly rise this morning, I was that bedeviled."

Caustic:

Bringing about a nervous reaction.

"Pettigrew's face twitched uncontrollably in response to Smythe's caustic remarks."

Decolonization:

A bowel movement.

"Mountbatten was in the lavatory, and I didn't wish to to disturb him during decolonization."

Edwardian:

A psychiatric unit inmate.

"That nutcase was locked up years ago, 'e was. 'E's an Edwardian."

Endocrine:

The cessation of tears.

"She's a bit weepy, but I've said we'll get this gland sorted out and that'll be the endocrine."

Endowment:

Relief from suffering.

"When her father finally dies, there'll be a considerable endowment."

Figurine:

Water passed after eating fleshy fruit.

"Here we have a figurine sample from Michelangelo."

Forensic:

Adjective referring to a nonindigenous disease.

"He died of German measles? Then this is a job for forensic science."

Foresight:

Double double vision.

"How many fingers?" "Eight. Am I going to jail?" "You certainly have foresight."

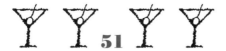

Gothic:

To have the hiccoughs.

"I don't understand you, are you speaking German?" "No, sorry, gothic."

Hemisphere:

Skirt edge phobia.

"I find that this hemisphere is not conducive to the wearing of dresses."

Henge:

A skin disease among chickens.

"Most peculiar. From their patchy plumage I'd say it was some sort of henge."

Illiterate:

To be sick after consuming cat's hygiene product.

"If you'd read what it says on the box you wouldn't be illiterate."

Kindred:

Fear of family members.

"He was shaking when that maniac son of his called by. He can't control his kindred."

Lentil:

Poor health due to fasting.

"Is he sick, doctor? He's not been eating. Shall I give him some soup?" "Lentil, I think."

Madrigal:

A fit of insane squirming.

"Well, I listened and I writhed in my seat, but she told me off and said it was a madrigal."

Marinade:

Medical help for sea travelers.

"The chef's got a crisis in the galley. He says can we get some marinade in there fast."

Melancholic:

A stomachache from eating too many cantaloupes.

"Just one more slice, or the consequence may be melancholic."

Nomad:

A sane person.

"Nomad, is he? Why can't he keep still then?"

Outward:

Hospital department for non-inpatients.

"How will I find Minor Injuries?" "Look for the outward signs."

Remember:

To replace limbs. The opposite of dismember.

"The man with no legs begged me to remember him."

Restaurant:

That which promotes the regrowth of hair.

"I'm tired of these baldies-only cafes. Maybe I should try a hair restaurant."

Restitution:

A convalescent hospital.

"Can you recommend any kind of restitution that might help to bring back my well-being?"

Revetment:

Another treatment at the animal hospital.

"Binky fell off the wall again, poor thing."
"Time for a revetment, then."

Rumpus:

A pimple on the behind.

"I've got an uncomfortable feeling that by sitting on the fence I've caused a rumpus."

Scabbard:

A poet suffering from chicken pox.

"His verse is as diseased as he is. You should stick a sword in that scabbard."

Senator‡:

One who deals in laxatives.

"Too many constipated folk on this committee. We need a senator who'll get things moving."

---

‡ *To the Puzzled American Reader:* Senator: Senna describes a group of leguminous herbs and shrubs, many of whose members are known for their purgative effect.

Sorghum:

A condition requiring dental treatment.

"I think the dog's got a sorghum. Must be that stick he's always chewing on."

Volte-face:

The removal of facial hair by electrolysis.

"I wasn't going to have my hair removed but now I've had a volte-face."

Wellies:

Those who are not sick.

"Both my assistants have hydrophobia. I wish I had a pair of wellies."

Wheedle:

Pot smoker's complaint.

"I know I should give it up. This wheedle be the death of me."

Wisteria:

A mania for playing cards.

"He even dealt himself hands by that creeper in the garden. Wisteria, they call it."

Xenophobic:

Afraid of Buddhists.

"I used to love Tibetans, but now I'm xenophobic."

Yoghurt:

An injury sustained while practicing yoga.

"I'm sorry I can't come jogging with you today. I've got yoghurt in my groin."

Yucca:

An expression of revulsion used by someone who abhors flora.

"Yucca plant."

Ecstatic:

That which was still but is now moving.

"Can you believe he got that old heap rolling? He's ecstatic."

Physical Properties

Explanatory:

In outer space.

"This book on the Voyager probes is full of explanatory text."

Fahrenheit:

A long way up.

"He said he was two degrees out, but it can't be fahrenheit."

Finite:

Good conditions in the hours of darkness.

"A fisherman's finite resources include a full moon and a calm sea."

Foursome:

Quadruply awesome.

"I've seen some great golf in my time, but that was totally foursome."

Gnostic:

A lack of adhesion.

"One thing I do know is that this glue's got gnostic."

Granulated:

Delayed by an elderly relative.

"I couldn't get your sugar lumps. I met your mother and her mother and got granulated."

Hepatitis:

Having seven udders.

"It's a shame we can't get some milk from that cow. She's got hepatitis."

Impervious:

Not susceptible to influence by perverts.

"What if that creep gets her drunk?" "Don't worry, she's impervious."

Impossible:

Not suitable for inclusion in a group of mounted cowboys.

"You'll never catch them on that three-legged mule. It's impossible."

Irrigation:

An annoyance caused by water.

"At first I liked the sound of the stream, but now it's more of an irrigation."

Karma:

Less agitated.

"You don't believe it's your destiny to be gored? Wave a red rag at a bull and see if it's karma."

Lavish:

Like a water closet.

"Her Majesty's throne room was quite like a regular bathroom—but certainly not lavish."

Legacy:

The result of breaking wind in one's trousers.

"I couldn't contain it and was left with an unfortunate legacy."

Listless:

Lacking a vital tool for shopping.

"I wouldn't have come to the store with you if I'd known you were going to be listless."

Magnesia:

The condition of having forgotten one's periodical.

"I went in there for Vogue *and laxative but came out with nothing but magnesia."*

Overwrought:

Excessively ornamented.

"Did you see those iron gates with Napoleon's silhouette on? He looked a bit overwrought."

Radish:

Fairly extreme.

"I've tasted some way-out vegetables in my time, man, but this is really radish."

Sanskrit:

Not yet reviewed.

"I've heard about it, but I haven't read about it. I gather it's sanskrit."

Sarong:

Incorrect in Italy.

"Ah, si, it's a like a long scarf, no? It's a right or it sarong?"

Unalterable:

Not fit for the communion table.

"I gave up polishing that dirty candlestick. It's just unalterable."

Uncared-for:

Looked after by an uncle.

"The boy's been spending too much time with your scruffy brother. He looks uncared-for."

Underfelt:

Failed to experience the appropriate emotion.

"So then he carpeted them but they underfelt it."

Unpalatable:

Incapable of being mounted on a small wooden platform.

"The truth is, it's too big. That's the unpalatable thing."

Vouchsafed:

Inaccessible to people with vouchers.

"Where can we dine in peace?" "The answer is somewhere vouchsafed."

Wakeful:

To feel sated in the morning.

"When I eat too many pies, I go to bed restless and wakeful."

Watershed:

To weep profusely.

"It was a watershed moment; I cried and cried over the crisis."

Wisdom:

Great speed.

"I thought he'd achieve escape velocity, but he lacked the wisdom."

Youthful:

Of service to someone with a lisp.

"I thuppothe we're going to keep the new gardener on. He theems wather youthful."

Manglos' actions

Affirmatory:

To vote for a right-winger.

"I said shall I cross your ballot paper by the left-winger? And his answer was affirmatory."

Banjo:

To exclude the average American.

"I don't want no Yankee guitar players in my club, just banjo."

Carrion:

To continue with what you were doing.

"Carrion, carrion, ignore it, it's only road kill."

Decalcify:

To put transfers on model aircraft.

"I can't make the roundels stick on that chalky-colored jet. You decalcify it."

Eunuch:

What you do before you enter.

"Let's get things in the right order. Eunuch first, then let the slave girls in."

Frighten:

To cook one less than eleven items in oil or butter.

"The hideous chef wanted to fix them a dozen eggs, but he could only frighten at once."

Indeed:

A fashionable activity.

"Oh she's doing that, is she? It's all the rage you know. Very trendy indeed."

Jackal‡:

To give everything up.

"Today I'm retiring. I'm calling it 'The Day of the Jackal'."

---

‡ *To the Puzzled American Reader:* Jackal: "Jack" in Britain may be used in the phrase "jack it in," meaning to put it down or throw it away or give up or quit a job.

Justify:

Only if or when (first person).

"It's justify move my head that it hurts."

Malingering:

Pointlessly hanging around a shopping arcade.

"She says she's too sick to leave the store, but I think she's malingering."

Outrage:

To display more fury.

"I thought I was upset, but I was thoroughly outraged by Velma."

Ovation:

Egg production.

"If that hen can lay without sitting down, she'll have a standing ovation."

Pulpit:

What to do with wood to make paper.

"What can I make with this timber?" "A lectern? Or pulpit maybe?"

Pumpkin:

To question relatives.

"Well you've got to pumpkin, otherwise you'll never find out who in this family is responsible."

Recede:

To self-propagate.

"We've planted a tree at the foot of the glacier; hopefully it'll recede in due course."

Remilitarize:

To provide more seed for budgerigars.

"Mussolini says even his birds have nothing to eat, and we must remilitarize."

Resin:

To commit a further offence.

"He'll either never take another puff of cannabis or go back to resin time and again."

Satin:

Entered and adopted a seated position.

"We met at the car; I wore silk and he satin."

Scampering:

Making noises to feign contentedness.

"The cat misses you. It's not even scampering like it used to."

Sequester:

To look further away from the East.

"If we can't find any for ourselves in China, we'll have to sequester some."

Sidewalk:

To move with a crablike motion.

"What's that hermit doing on the foot-path?" "Looks like a sidewalk to me."

Slovak:

To Hoover in a leisurely manner.

"I'll have a slovak round the apartment and clean it up a bit."

Textualist:

To send a written statement of shopping requirements by mobile phone.

"Textualist? Just get what you remember."

Throughout:

Expelled, ejected, or evicted.

"The Judge said the evidence was shaky, throughout the case, and went home."

Unbolted:

Ran back again.

"He's run off." "Dang it. We can't get in there until he's unbolted."

Unclinch:

To hang an uncle.

"If Ma's brother don't stop dancin' with her soon, I'm gonna unclinch him."

Volition:

The spontaneous combustion of a rodent.

"The smell of scorched fur was in fact of his own volition."

Vulcanized:

Made to look like Mr Spock.

"Do you think he's wearing rubber ears, or has he been vulcanized?"

Yellow:

To shout with pain.

"She did some blue, then she dropped the paint tin on my foot. After that all I did was yellow."

Sport,
Fashion,
Music

Ballerina:
A baseball stadium.

"Huge, absolutely vast. I've never seen such an immense ballerina before."

Cadillac:
The condition of having nobody to carry one's golf clubs.

"If I didn't have a cadillac I'd be driving off the first tee."

Deluge:

To be ejected from one's toboggan.

"Under a low, grey sky I hurtled into the final bend. But I left the track and was deluged."

Outspoken:

Beaten by someone with better bicycle wheels.

"You should pedal faster." "I disagree." "That's why you're outspoken."

Tentacle:

A defensive soccer move involving all the team except the goalkeeper.

"I didn't expect a tentacle on me in the box."

Voltmeter:

Instrument for measuring long jumps.

"That was an electrifying leap! The volt-meter went clean off the scale."

Wombat:

A female cricketer.

"She bowled the ball at ninety miles an hour at the opposition's unfortunate wombat."

Baptize‡:

Bread-roll-shaped neckwear for men.

"Baptize? Good idea. It'll impress his grandparents."

---

‡ *To the Puzzled American Reader:* Baptize: a bap is a roll or loaf or baguette.

Canticle:

The trouble with woolen socks.

"I'll lend you a pair of mine. But I'll warn you now, they canticle."

Cobra:

An undergarment for female Siamese twins.

"My sister and I usually have a cobra under our blouses."

Foolscap:

A dunce's hat.

"Say, is that an A4 envelope they've stuck on your head, or is it a foolscap?"

Handicap:

A useful hat.

"He's always wearing that Stetson, but I don't see it as a handicap."

Hermits:

Fingerless gloves for women.

"Your wife left these near those men who live on their own." "Yes, they're hermits."

Levite:

One who wears blue jeans.

"He's the scruffiest Levite I ever saw. I can't believe he dresses like that to go to the temple."

Outskirts:
Unfashionable dresses.

"She likes the hip new town center stores, and she won't be seen dead in no outskirts."

Pantisocracy:
A society which values its smalls.

"Stockings, knickers, and vests are equally important in our pantisocracy."

Pheasant:
A wearer of Turkish haberdashery.

"Aim at the men with the cylindrical hats on their heads. This is a pheasant (or turkey) shoot."

Reinvest:

A warm winter jacket worn by Santa's sled pullers.

"Reinvest for each of you. That's what Father Christmas has done."

Turbocharge:

Cloakroom fee for parking Eastern hats.

"You got that headgear back pretty quick, was there a turbocharge on it?"

Unaware:

Briefs for sloppy speakers.

"I wen' in the bedroom 'n' 'e was stannin' there in 'is unaware."

Zucchini:

A woman's two-part bathing costume for use at wildlife parks.

"I can't swim with the dolphins, I've got no zucchini."

Algorithm:

Beat favored by erstwhile Democratic presidential candidate.

"Groovy, Tipper, dig that algorithm."

Fortune:

A musical score for a string quartet.

"If only I could write something for these violinists I would make a fortune."

Rubicon:

A false jewel.

"Nobody sells paste gems to me. With that rubicon you crossed the line."

Holster‡:

One who enjoys musical suites such as "The Planets."

"Holsters are often associated with Mars the war bringer."

Liquidity:

Handel's water music or similar air.

"His plan is to write an opera but it has a liquidity attached to it."

---

‡ *To the Puzzled American Reader:* Holster: after Gustave Theodore Holst (1874–1934), composer. To the Patronized: Sorry if this insults your intelligence.

Nostrum:

Guitar playing prohibited.

"We think you'll find our silence cure is the best medicine. This is a nostrum area."

Oddity:

A peculiar song.

"To be frank, I considered 'The Ballad of Wilbert Smails' to be something of an oddity."

Sheriff:

Solo performed by female guitarist.

"The piece she played in London wasn't as good as the sheriff of Nottingham."

Thong:

A ditty from a lisping performer.

"Now I'm going to thing you a thong about the theven deadly thins."

Pontoon:

A sailor's ditty.

"Take up your squeezebox, matey, and give us a pontoon!"

Nostril:

A musical embellishment sung nasally.

"It wasn't the endless choruses that drove me belowdecks, but his many nostrils."

Church and Elsewhere

Alternative:

Born to be a man of the cloth.

"Well, he ain't the ideal priest for us, but then we don't have an alternative."

Aspire:

A part of a church or cathedral.

"Aspire is what we can do if we wish to please God, fellow masons."

Cantilever:

The suggestion that a man might divorce his wife.

"Cantilever?" "No, he could never afford the alimony."

Daring:

A vital part of a West Indian wedding ceremony.

"Okay, mon, who's got daring?"

Decongest:

To joke, when the joker is a senior clergyman.

"Some say he's a stuffy churchman, but I found him quick to decongest."

Enunciate:

To join a convent.

"She wanted folk to know she was taking holy orders. Her wish was to be very clearly enunciated."

Herbicide:

A wife or female partner.

"God said to Adam, 'This is Eve; I shall not leave you in the garden without herbicide.'"

Herring:

A wife's gold wedding band.

"You're the best man—you were supposed to have brought herring."

Herself:

Mythical sprite that accompanies the coffin in a funeral cortege.

"He's dead and she's only herself to blame."

Hispanics:

Feeling of best man on forgetting her ring.

"If it weren't for hispanics, we'd have been married in Majorca."

Inaccurate:

Residing within a minor clergyman.

"The article says the bullet missed a churchgoer, but sadly it's inaccurate."

Marigold:

To wed a rich spouse.

"My advice to you, son, is marigold. It really doesn't matter what color she is."

Monkey:

Pertaining to the monastic life.

"He looks like a good friar, doesn't he?"
"More monkey, I should say."

Paedobaptism:

A little accident at the font.

"I'm so sorry about the paedobaptism. I think it was all the water that set him off."

Unbridle:

Not befitting a woman at her wedding.

"Unbridle that. You can't arrive at your wedding on a horse!"

Uncoupled:

Divorced.

"I know you're eager to get hitched, but you'll have to wait until those two are uncoupled first."

Vicarious:

Like a clergyman in a dangerous position.

"I don't see how the reverend can enjoy it—it seems quite vicarious."

Turns of phrase and bits of kit

Abysmal:

A little chasm.

"What's that hole, Dad, could you fall down there?" "Why yes son, that would be abysmal."

Dramatic:

A storage loft for whisky.

"He got drunk and fell from some sort of platform." "Aye, dramatic, I should think."

Outbuilding:

The location of a construction worker.

"Where's Bob?" "Outbuilding, most likely."

Palindrome:

A private airport for the use of old *Monty Python* stars.

"Aha! This is a palindrome! There's Michael's plane."

Penitentiary:

A budget camping-equipment shop.

"He can live out of a rucksack. He's spent half his life in a penitentiary."

Rheumatic:

Of a loft conversion or garret.

"I hate living in the top of that drafty old house. It's like a rheumatic pain."

 ## Telepath:

The worn area of carpet between the TV and the sofa.

"I just know there'll be another telepath there soon."

Warden:

Command bunker during conflict.

"Everything was going fine until a bomb flattened the warden."

Arcane:

A walking stick owned in partnership.

"Review the paperwork if you like, but be warned: it's arcane."

Arsenal:

Also having a bottom.

"Look at all the guns that huge fat guy's got!" "Yes, and he's got quite an arsenal."

Beckon:

A South African event that was canceled but will now take place after all.

"The criggit metch? Yis, it's beckon agen."

Cauldron:

What Nancy Reagan often did.

"*You should have told me, I could have cauldron at the White House.*"

Dynasty:

To come to a grisly end.

"*I don't like those Ming. One of these days the headline's gonna be 'Ming Dynasty.'*"

Edam:

Expletive conveyed by electronic mail.

"*I don't care if he is a big cheese, I'm gonna send him an edam.*"

Gibberish:

The language of Gibraltar.

"I said, 'Can you tell us about the rock scene?' and he started spouting gibberish."

Gosling:

Advice given to David before confronting Goliath.

"OK, son, pick a good stone and gosling, then duck."

Hectare:

Mild expletive used by paratroopers.

"I need to come left a bit to hit this little landing zone. It's only a—oh, hectare."

Jihad:

If only.

"Jihad I known it would start a holy war, I'd never have said it."

Quadrangle:

Argument involving four participants.

"There's two of us and two of them. Let's duke it out in a quadrangle."

Quadrant:

A speech given in a courtyard.

"Today's quadrant concerns the significance of 45 degrees of arc."

Repercussions:

Harvest worker's swear words.

"You can tell them to get the corn cut quicker but there'll be repercussions."

Wafer:

Direction to.

"Is this the right wafer the Empire State building?"

Wattle:

Question intended to establish purpose.

"Wattle those interwoven sticks be used for, then?"

Xenon:

Observed in the context of.

"Get yourself some of this excellent heavy inert gas, as xenon TV."

Yeoman:

Greeting sometimes heard among African Americans.

"Yeoman, wassup?"

Yugoslav:

Suggestion that someone of Balkan origin should leave.

"Did you say he was Russian?" "I'm not asking." "Yugoslav."

Adore:

Like agate but more solid.

"He's bending down and peering through her letterbox." "Yes, he's inclined to adore."

Adolescent‡:

A free perfume sample.

"Something for the mature woman, sir?" "Well, adolescent would be nice."

---

‡ To the Puzzled American Reader: **Adolescent:** Dole = cash dispensed to unemployed citizens by the government. Or doled out to a half-feral child by a doleful parent.

Batholith:

A stone found in the tub after the water has drained out.

"When the level dropped we found a batholith in there."

Enchilada:

A refrigerator.

"This meat is really hot. It should be put in an enchilada."

Fabric:

An excellent haystack.

"Does it have to be a straw hat? Maybe we can make something out of that fabric."

Fern:

A French telephone.

"Monsieur Bellamy ze botanist? Fern for you, monsieur."

Flamboyant:

A floating candle.

"I do like to have a flamboyant in my bath with me."

Knapsack:

A sleeping bag.

"He was a short man. At night he got into his knapsack and went to sleep."

Navigate:

Tradesman's entrance.

"Where do I deliver this lot?" "Navigate round the back, mate."

Nodule:

A drip shaken from the end of the nose by a movement of the head.

"Get a tissue and wipe up that nodule."

Odometer:

Instrument for measuring peculiarity.

"You don't need an odometer to see he's nuts. He's running round with a wheel on a stick!"

Omnipresence:

Gifts suitable for all occasions.

"Or a bouquet. You can always count on the omnipresence."

Penultimate:

Top-of-the-range writing implement.

"It's a beautiful ballpoint, sir: the penultimate, and my second last in stock."

Porcine:

An inadequate indicator.

"Your 'Sheep Farm' notice looks more like a pig." "Oh. Porcine then, huh?"

Quack:

Dangerous drug identified by Tweety Pie.

"Twy some? Are you quazy? Jesus Quist, that's quack cocaine!"

Soubriquet:

Native American charcoal.

"You got anything I can keep this barbecue going with?" "I may have the odd soubriquet."

Telecaster:

One of the little wheels on a television.

"And then the whole TV tipped forward and the telecaster fell right out!"

Terrapin:

A tent peg.

"We look after our animals at this circus. Now fetch me some terrapins to hold the big top up."

Weasel:

A work stand for asthmatic painters.

"I'm gasping to paint wildlife—I really must find my weasel."

Zulus:

Lavatories at the animal sanctuary.

"We enjoyed the lions, but can you tell us where the zulus are?"

MANGLO MISCELLANY

ARCADE:

A charity for boat people.

"Surely the best way to help the refugees is to introduce them to this arcade."

DISENTANGLE:

An opposing viewpoint.

"Let's look at this from another perspective for a moment. Who's gotta disentangle?"

FOREBEARS:

One more than encountered by Goldilocks.

"There wasn't enough porridge to feed all forebears, so one of them died."

FORLORN:

Intended primarily for use on grass.

"You can use fertilizer to cheer up any part of your garden, it needn't be just forlorn."

FULMINATE:

No less than sixty seconds.

"Let the patient lie in the bath for a fulminate before proceeding."

GERMINATING:

Disliking people of Teutonic origin.

"England football fans are like weeds. You can't stop them germinating."

GRUESOME:

Successfully cultivated.

"They say you can't raise vegetables in a graveyard, but I knew someone gruesome."

HALLOO:

A lavatory in the corridor.

"The bright yellow bathroom is on the left. It's nice to be greeted by a cheery halloo."

HEGEMONY:

Fund for shrub maintenance.

"This state's got the most bushes so it should contribute most to the hegemony."

INAUGURATE:

To perforate with a wood-boring tool.

"If I catch that lousy bastard I'll fill him full of holes. Hell, I'll inaugurate him!"

INCANDESCENT:

The migration of South American peoples down from the mountains.

"See that torchlit procession? It's incandescent."

INCONVENIENCE:

To be stuck in the lavatory.

"Her backside was trapped in the bowl. She was seriously inconvenienced."

KETCHUP:

To increase pace in South Africa.

"In the Cape, we plant tomatoes late and then make them ketchup."

LOCOMOTIVE:

An insane reason for doing something.

"She said a new job would get her out of town, but I thought it was a locomotive."

MENIAL:

Greeting to be used by the first man on the moon in the event of meeting an alien.

"Menial. Who you?"

MOCCASIN:

Overindulgence in coffee.

"We had two cups and played footsie under the table. What's a little moccasin between friends?"

NOBLESSE:

Approval withheld.

"If you insist on marrying that Protestant aristocrat I'm afraid it'll be noblesse for you."

NOISETTE:

A faint sound.

"I thought I heard a noisette." "It's just the meat frying."

OPIATE:

To wish that a male friend has already dined.

"I can't cook for him, I'm out of my skull. I do opiate."

PARACETAMOL:

What happens when you give chocolates to airborne troops.

"In this plane you give out truffles and paracetamol."

PHOTOSYNTHESIS:

An academic paper concerning immoral images.

"That photosynthesis was enough to make my plants turn green."

POMEGRANATE:

Quartz building stone shipped to Australia from England.

"The Melbourne town hall is made entirely from pomegranate."

PORPOISE:

A slovenly posture.

"She'll never be a supermodel if she takes a porpoise onto the catwalk with her."

QUARTET:

Just under two pints.

"How much water is sloshing about in there, do you think? " "Sounds like a quartet."

SCHEDULE:

Christmas in the outhouse.

"Your father's wrapping presents in the lean-to. It's part of his schedule."

SENILE:

The usual reason for visiting Egypt.

"I don't know why the old guy suddenly took off for Cairo." "Hm. Senile perhaps."

SILICON:

A ridiculous scam.

"It's silicon time. Surely those are comedy breasts?"

TERRACOTTA:

Nightmares.

"The baby's crying again. Sometimes I almost feel I could hit him with this vase. It's just terracotta."

UNDERSIGNED:

Lacking clear directions.

"Can you confirm that it's difficult to locate?" *"Yes, I guess you could call it undersigned."*

VAGRANT:

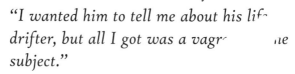

A rambling tirade.

"I wanted him to tell me about his lif~ drifter, but all I got was a vagr~ ~ne subject."

VENTRICLE:

Leakage in an air conditioning unit.

"Feels like something's dripping on my chest." "Could be a ventricle problem."

The author would like to thank M. Spencer, J. D. Young, and all at Pomegranate for their contributions to this book.